My Favorite

by Donna DeMaio Hunt

Illustrated by Ethan Hunt

© Copyright 2024

All rights reserved. No part of this book may be reproduced, stored in a retrieval system or transmitted in any form or by any means without the prior written permission of the author and publisher. Quotes of brief passages may be reproduced in a newspaper, magazine or journal for reviews only.

This book was printed in the United States of America.

ISBN: 9798335408479   Soft Cover

WHAT IS MINDFULNESS?

Mindfulness is something we use to help us focus on relaxing our bodies and minds to reduce feelings of discomfort. There are many times when we feel uncomfortable, and by practicing mindfulness we can escape to our happy place when those uncomfortable feelings overwhelm us. Think of 3 happy places that you can escape to, in your own mind, while closing your eyes and breathing in through your nose and out through your mouth.

When I am lost and I feel scared, my tummy doesn't feel so good.

My mind races quickly to my tent,

In the middle of my back yard.

I look up at the great big stars,

I think that I saw Mars.

I think of fire and crackling wood, and

Marshmallows on a stick.

When I open up my eyes,

I don't feel so sick.

This is my favorite place to be...
when I feel scared, or horribly.

I feel angry and my body shakes when kids are mean to me.

My mind floats to the sea,

Where the sea turtles came to be.

I play for hours in the sand,

The oceans waves will fall and stand.

Collecting shells of every kind,

So many treasures to search and find.

Sky as far as I can see,

My body finally feels carefree.

This is my favorite place to see....

when someone is mean to me.

I feel left out and lonely when kids won't share with me.

I quickly run to grandma's house,

I see her smiling face.

And as she laughs and lifts me up,

She is my saving grace.

We share a nice cold glass of milk,

Her fresh baked apple pie.

I never feel lonely,

When I'm at my grandma's side.

This is my favorite place to be...

when somebody won't share with me.

I get frustrated when I don't get what I want, and I just want to scream.

My mind pedals quickly to the park,

Riding bikes until it's dark.

Sharing all my special things,

And all the joy that friendship brings.

Jumping rope and singing loud,

Making sense of every cloud.

As I'm lying in the fields,

My frustration finally yields.

This is my favorite place to play...

even when I don't get my way.

My best friend didn't invite me to her party. I am disappointed, and I cry because I am sad.

My mind flies to the open field,

The skies so wide above.

I can see for miles in front of me,

As I fly this kite I love.

I feel the wind against my face,

I breathe the cool fresh air.

I was no longer feeling sad,

As the wind blew through my hair.

This is my favorite place to fly my kite high.... even if someone makes me cry.

Thunderstorms frighten me.

My heart beats fast.

I rocket to the stars above,

The planets all around.

I can almost touch the moon,

Not one single sound.

I sit and watch a shooting star,

Guided by its light.

I notice that I'm feeling calm,

I'm suddenly alright.

My favorite place is up in space...

when my heart begins to race.

I get mad when my mom says no.

I can feel my face get hot.

My mind flurries like the snow,
Building the biggest snowman I know.
Two button eyes, a carrot nose,
Don't even mind my frozen toes.

Catching snowflakes on my tongue,
The snow is deep as it slows my run.
Distracted by my frozen braids,
My face feels cool, my anger fades.

This is my favorite place to go....

Usually when my mom says no.

Where is your favorite place to be

when you are sad?

When you are angry, or you are mad?

Where is your favorite place to see?

When you are nervous, scared,

or you worry?

What is your favorite thing to do?

When you are afraid or feeling blue?

Where is your favorite place to go?

I would really like to know!

Made in the USA
Columbia, SC
24 October 2024